Huffmaster-Hofmeister Family From 1500 to 2009

Novello
COMPLIED BY
Rettie Virginia Farrell

With
Excerpts from the 1922
James T. Huffmaster
Huffmaster-Hoffmeister
Family Records

iUniverse, Inc.
New York   Bloomington

HOFFMEISTER/HUFFMASTER
FAMILY RECORDS 2009
A Novella of the old and the new.

iUniverse books may be ordered through booksellers or by contacting:

iUniverse
1663 Liberty Drive
Bloomington, IN 47403
www.iuniverse.com
1-800-Authors (1-800-288-4677)

ISBN: 978-1-4401-3352-7 (pbk)
ISBN: 978-1-4401-3353-4 (ebk)

Printed in the United States of America

iUniverse rev. date: 4/9/2009

Contents

Forward

In this link that ties the generations together, you may notice what appear to be duplications of copy. As, indeed, you should. That is the procedure I have used to highlight changes and upgrade the story of the Hoffmeister/ Huffmaster family. In that of Hoffmeister/Huffmaster, the link goes back to the 1500's. Augusta Hoffmeister sat with the tribunal that tried Martin Luther when he rebelled again the Catholic Church.

We have come a long way and much history has been lost. We still remain a link with the past now in this 8th., 9th.,and 10th. generation of the Hoffmeister line from Germany.

I am the 6th. generation of that link and the last living person of that generation. My mother and father were hard working farm people who were the parents of 3 boys and 4 girls. I remember so clearly, today at 80 years old, most of the life of my parents and sisters and brothers. It was not an easy life. In each house where my parents lived, there was a fire. I specifically remember the last house that burned. Yet, being the strong family we are, a rebuilding and reuniting of the links continued.

How can we understand what happened in Germany to cause our people to immigrate. My grandfather, seven generations removed was the first one to reach American soil. He was 17 years old. We know that he and his brother Franz wrote and published music with Mozart and Beethoven. We know they struggled against warriors in the Austrian/Germany conflict. Yet in all my searches, I have not been able to locate the names of their parents, only that their parents are unknown. We cannot imagine just what they thought and why they wanted away from there.

It is just by God's will that we have lived and linked from the 1500's to the year 2008, and more time will come. Our link will continue to live as long as there is a world.

Now, I leave you with "God's Blessings" for those Hoffmeister/Huffmaster beneficiaries and for the future generations.

And for the little bit of Irish in me:

Traditional Irish Blessing

May the road rise to meet you
May the wind be always at your back
The sun shine warm upon your face
The rains fall soft upon your fields
And until we meet again,
May God hold you in the hollow of his hand

Introduction

The following records have been compiled over many generations of the Huffmaster-Hoffmeister family.

The first pages contain actual copy of the original book published in 1922 by James T. Huffmaster. This information pertains to the genealogy which relates to my current family as descendant of the 6th generation

The James T. Huffmaster records cover from the Year of the first immigrant of the family from Germany through a partial record of the 6th generation.

Huffmaster's compilation was prior to the birth of the current author, therefore making the records ending in the early 1920's.

It has been a very interesting journey to collect still further information regarding our family, both prior to the immigration and up until the date of publication in 2009.

I have had printed some photographs, especially of the 7th generation. My siblings and I were of the union of Hal Harland Huffmaster and Rettie George. We were 3 sons and 4 daughters, I being the youngest of the 7 and the only living one.

I will be 81 years old in April, 2009; have been widowed since 1980. From the union of Thomas Farrell and myself we are parents of 2 sons and 3 daughters. There are now many grandchildren. I cherish them all and the memories left behind.

January, 2009
Huffmaster-Hoffmeister
Family Records
Compiled by:
James T. Huffmaster
1922
Excerpts from the 1922 writings of James T. Huffmaster.

Family tradition indicates that our ancestor held the position of Hofmeister, (which in English is Court master), under Charlemagne (786 to 814 A. D.). The title followed him afterwards as a surname.

Up to the late war the courts of Germany and Austria had their official Hofmeister, a position of dignity and importance.

FiRST GENERATION
Godlove Huffmaster

Gottlieb Hoffmeister arrived in America about 1776, and settled in Shenandoah County, Virginia. He was born about 1757, in the vicinity of Frankfort on the Main in Germany. He changed the spelling of his name to Godlove Huffmaster; was married June 12, 1781, to Sarah Louderback, who was born February 18, 1764. Their children were all born in Virginia, but all moved to Hawkins County, Tennessee, where he bought land in 1810. He and his wife died about 1844. His will is on record at Rogersville.

Two sons of Gottlieb were killed by a stroke of lightning.

LOUDERBACK

Johan David Lauterbach arrived at Philadelphia from Rotterdam on the ship Samuel, Hugh Percy, Commander. He was twenty-three years of age and unmarried. He "qualified" or took the oath of allegiance on August 27, 1789. He settled in Virginia, and his name was there after spelled David Louderback. He married Elizabeth in Shenandoah County, VA. The Louderback's had 6 sons and 6 daughters one of which, Sarah, born February 18, 1764 and married Godlove Huffmaster in 1781. A son, Joseph was born April 4, 1782 and married Elizabeth Weitzel.

SECOND GENERATION

Joseph, son on Gottlieb and Elizabeth was born April 4, 1782 and married Elizabeth Weitzel, December 8, 1808. He was in the war of 1812, under Gen'l Andrew Jackson in a campaign against the Creek Indiana, which ended in their complete defeat at the Battle of Horse Shoe Bend. He was commissioned a captain in the Militia, was Justice of the Peace, entry taker for Public Lands, elder in the Presbyterian Church for many years. Elizabeth was born August 27, 1787 and died February 16, 1872. Joseph died April 3, 1874. His will is recorded in Rogersville, Hawkins County, Tennessee. The homesite in Rogersville was purchased in 1809. He was pensioned by the U.S. Government. Elizabeth is believed to be related to Lewis Wetzel, Indian fighter of Virginia. Joseph and Elizabeth had 13 children, one of which was Richard Mitchell, born April 23, 1820.

FOURTH GENERATION

Richard Mitchell Huffmaster, Son of Joseph and Elizabeth Huffmaster married Mary F. Shanks, June 19, 1842. They moved to Springdale, Arkansas after the Civil War. Mr. Huffmaster was an estimable citizen. He served as Mayor of Springdale; was a Justice of the Peace; an elder in the Presbyterian Church and and a member of the Odd Fellow Fraternity. He died February 23, 1899. Mary was born May 22, 1824 and died July 9, 1865. Richard and Mary had 9 children, the last one being John Martin, born December 1, 1856. He married Lydia W. Pearson.

FIFTH GENERATION

John Martin Huffmaster born December 1, 1856; married Lydia Warren Pearson, September 14 1880. She was born April 16, 1860. They resided in Springdale, Arkansas. John Martin and Lydia Warren were the parents of 10 children. The third child was my father, Hal Harland, born June 12, 1885 and Married Rettie George.

SIXTH GENERATION

Hal Harland born June 12, 1885 the third child of John Martin and Lydia Pearson, married Rettie George, July 8, 1906 in Elm Springs, Arkansas. Rettie was born September 2, 1886 in Texas.

Hal and Rettie were the parents of 7 children.
John William, born May 8, 1907.
Sarah Lydia Mabel, born August 30, 1909.
Lelia Opal, born January 2, 1912.

Helen Ruby, born March 18, 1914,
Martin Harland, born June 12, 1916
Jessie Barnett, born December 8, 1919
(Not mentioned in James T. Huffmaster's record)
Rettie Virginia, born April 27, 1928.
Beginning of Current Author's work.

Recognition of Assistants and Contributors

It is with great pleasure that I have been able to research and publish this work about our family's past. There were some unfortunate items that have been hidden that I was not able to obtain. Those whom I cannot locate are the parents of the two brothers, Gottlieb and Franz who were the first to immigrate to America. The only reference to the parents is that they are recorded as unknown.

I found it to be very interesting that the brothers were both publishers and authors of classical music during the period of Beethoven and Mozart. I have been able to locate many musical compositions by Franz Anton Hoffmeister recorded and published by later artists. Those include:

Hoffmeister, Mozart: Duos for Violin and Viola by Franz Anton Hoffmeister, Wolfgang Amadeus Mozart, Alan Bodman, and Amy Barlowe

Sergei Nakariakov / Haydn, Hoffmeister, Mendelssohn: Concertos for Trumpet by Franz Joseph Haydn, Franz Anton Hoffmeister, Felix Mendelssohn, Jorg Faeber, and Jörg Faerber

There are many more compositions that have been recorded and published by later artists, but too many to mention. You may find them on a web-site for classical compositions by Franz Hoffmeister.

I wish to thank the following for the help and contributions given to me to complete this phase of the Hoffmeister-Huffmaster genealogy: Liz Glasco for editing, Helen Henderson for photos, Darlene Martindale, Francis Huffmaster, Jimmy Burton who all have supplied information to be included in the genealogy of the Hoffmeister/Huffmaster family. I especially want to thank my dearest family who has had unfailing patience with me during the writing.

Although there are many 9th and 10th generations not included, I send a challenge to whomever would go forward with these records. In this writing, I have documented back to the 1700's. The newer generations compilation should be much easier.

Hoffmeister-Huffmaster Records, 2009

Author: R. Virginia Farrell nee Huffmaster

PRELEMINIARY I

My hope is that some of the mysteries of the family will enlighten the coming generations so these records can be carried forward as the professional uncover further records, particularly in Germany.

This work is privileged only as far as the author ownership of the Library of Congress Certificate and the Copy Right. Any person finding the information useful may research from the information but may not copy unless specific permission is given by the Author or that of her descendants.

James Huffmaster claims in his record that Hoffmeister was involved with Charlemagne. Although I have been unable to find the link with Hofmeister and Charlemagne, I did find a reference to a Homiest (familiarity with, where Hofmeister was introduced in a search link.)

Following the website for Hofmeister and Charlemagne, some interesting facts were found and translated into the English language from the French, Latin and German Dialects. This site includes a copy of Charlemagne's will. It seems from this document that Charlemagne had much to do with the Roman Catholic Church. It was because of his deeds as ruler that many Franks left Germany. Among them were Gottlieb Hofmeister who left Germany and came to American around 1776-1781. It is evident that Martin Luther abdicated the Roman Church because of some of the deeds Charlemagne professed. Among those were the many concubines he had when the Church strictly forbade this practice. Other records show as many as 10 from which Charlemagne produced about 20 children in addition to those produced with his wife. In the case of forbidding extra-marital affairs, that rules goes back to the teaching of Pope Hernaid. Charlemagne-King-furnished a summary of the life of Charles the Great with a time line: http://prodigy.com/charlemagne.

PRELIMINARY II

It is, also, necessary that this 2008 publication refer to the 1922 record in many instances to show the connection to the current ancestry. Not all the data of the 1922 record will be used. The exception is the use of those directly related to the immediate family.

After several years of gathering information, this still is not a complete record of the Huffmaster family. I have spent many hours over the last five years searching and compiling records. Mostly from the Website of Ancestry.com.

There are many Huffmaster families widely scattered in the mix of today's civilization. Most of these are not related to our roots except through strains that broke away from the original family. Because of the mix of civilization many records have been lost or have never existed. Many Huffmaster families have been contacted.

On the following pages, starting with the First generation, Gottlieb Godlove Hoffmeister through the Fourth Generation of Richard Mitchell for the most part are taken from the Huffmaster Family Records, 1922, James T. Huffmaster. The first generation shows when Gottlieb Hoffmeister arrived in America from Germany, his birthdate, place, marriage date, spouses name, where he settled, moved and died.

Huffmaster Family Records
(Hofmeister)
Taken from Book written in 1922.
Author James T. Huffmaster
(Current Author's information in Italics.)

Family tradition indicates that our ancestor held the position of Hofmeister, (which in English is Courtmaster), under Charlemagne (786 to 814 A. D.). The title followed him afterwards as a surname. Up to the late war the courts of Germany and Austria had their official Hofmeister, a position of dignity and importance.

James T. Huffmaster was the son of James Weitzel Huffmaster. James Weitzel Huffmaster was the son of Joseph Huffmaster who was the son of Gottlieb (Godlove) Hofmeister. He was the brother of Richard Mitchell Huffmaster who was the author's great grandfather.

James T. Huffmaster further relates: The gathering of the family records found in the present work has been a task of many years. It is to be regretted that many names are wanting, but the hope is indulged in that all the descendants will at least be enabled to trace their early ancestry by means of this small volume.

Further information about Gottlieb Hoffmeister from several sources.

Gottlieb Hoffmeister was born about 1757 in Frankfor AM Main, Hessen-Nassau, Preussen and died 1844 in Rogersville, Hawkins, Tennessee.

The first generation shows when Gottlieb Hoffmeister arrived in America from Germany, his birthdate and place, marriage date and spouses name. It shows where he settled, where he moved and died, in about 1844. It is also recorded that Gottlieb had a brother Franz who also immigrated to America. Their parents are unknown.

Gottlieb Hoffmeister Year: 1781 Place: Virginia Source Publication Code: 7340.10 Primary Immigrant: Hoffmeister, Gottlieb Annotation: Date and place of settlement, death, transfer, desertion, leave, or other mention in North America. Year and place of birth, postal code of town or village, name of regiment or battalion, company in regiment or battalion, and military rank are also pro Source Bibliography: REUTER, CLAUS. Brunswick Troops in North America 1776-1783, Index of all Soldiers who Remained in North America. Bowie, MD: Heritage Books, Inc., 1999. 94p. Page: 36

From the Pennsylvania Historical Society, Source Bibliography: SCHWALM, MARK A. "A Composit List of German Prisoners of war held by the Americans, 1779-1782."

Franz Hoffmeister was born between 1752 -1753 in Grossalmerode, Kassel, Hessen-Nassau, Preussen. He died after 1810. His spouse in unknown.

From F & M College Library, Special Collections, Johannes Schwalm Historical Association Collection. He immigrated to America in 1776 at Trenton, New Jersey. Information provided among Bradford paper in the archives of the Pennsylvania Historical Society.

Franz was wounded and captured at the Battle of Trenton, December 16, 1776, have served in Co. 1 of the Rall Regt. After the battle he was moved to Philadelphia. There is a space where there is no knowledge of his wherabouts until December, 1780. It is believed that he may have been moved to Lancaster, Pennsylvanis with the other Trenton POWs then to Winchester, Virginia in August-September, 1777 and from there to Frederick, Maryland.

On December 18, 1780 he was transferred from Frederick, Maryland to the Goal at Philadelphia. He spent the next 16 months either in the vicinity of Philadelphia or in the Goal itself. On April 17, 1782, he was "farmed out" to work on a plantation in the vicinity of Philadelphia where two weeks later on April 29, he ran away. It is not known where he went but seems logical that he returned to Maryland where he spent time as a POW. According to Census reports from 1790-1810 it is recorded that these years were spent in Washington, Maryland.

He was the father of John Hoffmaster, born about 1785 in Maryland who died after 1830 and George Hofmeister, Sr., born December 1794 in Loudoun

Virginia and died April 1870 in Jefferson Virginia. More on Franz, Page 36.

On the following pages starting with the First Generation, Gottlieb Godlove Huffmaster through the Fourth Generation of Richard Mitchell Huffmaster taken from the Huffmaster Family Records, 1922, James T. Huffmaster.

Huffmaster Family Records

(Hofmeister) Author: James T. Huffmaster, 1922

FIRST GENERATION *(from JTH, 1922 writing)*

Godlove Huff master RVF revision: (according to recent information gained re: Godlove Huffmaster, the name in this First generation should have been Gottlieb)

Gottlieb Hoffmeister arrived in America about 1776, and settled in Shenandoah County, Virginia. He was born about 1757 in the vicinity of Frankfort on the Main in Germany.

He changed the spelling of his name to Godlove Huffmaster; was married June 12, 1781 to Sarah Louderback, born February 18 1764. Their children were all born in Virginia, but all moved to Hawkins County, Tennessee, where he bought land in 1819. He and his wife died about 1844. His will is on record at Rogersville, Tennessee.

This is the point where my research differs from James T. Huffmaster's records of 1922. The following information is current according to this date in April,

2008 gathered from the following sources by this author.

Ancestry Records from Ancestry.com show that : Gottlieb Hoffmeister : Immigrated to America in 1781 Age: 33 Estimated Birth Year: abt 1748 Place: Gottlieb Huffmaster records are found in World Family Tree, Volume 43, Tree 319. General location: Unknown, Date: 1700-1799. Gottlieb Huffmaster was born at Frankfurt, Hesse N. Germany in 1757. Virginia Source Publication Code: 8560 Primary Immigrant: Hoffmeister, Gottlieb Annotation: From the Staatsarchiv at Wolfenbuettel, Germany, where file 38B Alt. Nr. 260 is a summary list of Brunswick mercenaries sent to America in British service during the American Revolution. The detachment served mainly in Canada and northern New York. Most of the soldiers were captured at Saratoga and spent the war years as prisoners of war in Pennsylvania and Virginia, where many subsequently settled. The records supply name of the German birthplaces, thereby documenting the link between Germany and America for these elusive settlers. Some 3,000 did not return to Germany. Source Bibliography: SMITH, CLIFFORD NEAL, of the American Revolution. (German-American Genealogical Research Monograph, 1.) Thomson, IL: H. House, 1973.

In the State of Virginia, 1781 Gottlieb Hoffmeister,

Permanent Entry number 4708620 in recorded REUTER, CLAUS. Brunswick Troops in North America 1776-1783, Index of all Soldiers who remained in North America. Bowie, MD: Heritage Books, inc. 1999

It has been found convenient to give the descendants of Joseph and John separately. Only fifteen descendants of the other children have been found. *Two sons were killed by lightning.*

Joseph Huffmaster is the lineage to be followed in this book. It is believed that he is Great-grand Father of my Father. The next recording in James T. Huffmaster, 1922 writing has to do with the spouse of Gottlieb Huffmaster. Her name was: Sarah Lauterbach.

*In my research, I found some of the missing information regarding the Louderback family. Johan David Lauterbach (John David Louderback) was born in 1716 at: Frankfort, Hessen, Prussia. His parents were Johannes Ludwig Lauterback and Anna Margretha Gratzman. He married *Maria Elizabeth Klein, born 1720 at: Shenandoah, Virginia.*

Johan David Lauterbach arrived at Philadelphia from Rotterdam on the ship Samuel, Hugh Percy, Commander. He was twenty three years of age and unmarried. He "qualified" or took the oath of allegiance on August 17, 1789. He settled in Virginia, and his name was thereafter spelled David Louderback. He married Elizabeth (no surname given) and their home was in Shenadoah County, Va. He was born in 1716 and died in 1793. His will is recorded in the county.

David Lauterbach and Elizabeth had 6 sons and 6 daughters, among which are a son Joseph, a daughter Sarah and a son Godlove Huff master (James Huffmaster recalls that Godlove Huffmaster was killed by lighting.)

This Following information seems to disclaim that of James Huffmaster and his opinion that Gottlieb Huffmaster changed his name to Godlove Huffmaster. (from James Huffmaster's Huffmaster/Hoffmeister: " Gottlieb Hoffmeister arrived in America about 1776, and settled in Shenandoah County, Virginia. He was born about 1757, in the vicinity of Frankfort on the Main in Germany. He changed the spelling of his name to Godlove Huffmaster;) Actually, Godlove Huffmaster was the son of Gottlieb Hoffmeister. It does seem likely that Godlove was struck and killed by lightning as James Huffmaster said.

More about Gottlieb Huffmaster and Sarah Louderback.

SECOND GENERATION

Children of Godlove and Sarah Louderback Huffmaster *(should be Gottlieb)*

*Joseph born April 4, 1782, in Shenandoah, Virginia, Married Elizabeth Weitzel December 8, 1808

Barbara, born Aug. 23, 1785 in Shenandoah, Virginia. She married John Cline.

Mary, born July 17, 1787 in Shenandoah, Virginia. She married George White

John born Oct. 31, 1789 in Shenandoah, Virginia, died November 15, 1861, He married Elizabeth Hill, born December 18, 1818. of Rogersville, Hawkins County, Tennessee,

Daniel born June 22, 1792 in Shenandoah, Virginia. He married Sarah King.

Sarah born September 23, 1795 in Shenandoah, Virginia married Nathan White

Godlove, born June 11, 1798, in Shenandoah, Virginia. Died when struck by lightning. Unmarried.*

Jonathan, Born February 27, 1801 in Shenandoah, Virginia, married Sarah West.

Elizabeth, born July 20, 1803 in Shenandoah, Virginia, married Ezekiel Creech.

THIRD GENERATION

Mr. & Mrs. Joseph Huffmaster
Joseph Huffmaster   Elizabeth Huffmaster nee Weitzel
*Joseph Huff master , son of Gottlieb and Sarah) 1835 41 Private 59.1 Commissioner of a court house in the town of Rogersville, Tennessee, is the lineage to be followed in this book.

Joseph married Elizabeth Weitzel, December 8, 1808.

He was in the war of 1812, under Gen'l Andrew Jackson, which ended in their complete defeat at the Battle of Horse Shoe Bend. He was commissioned a captain in the Militia, was Justice of the Peace, entry taker for Public Lands, Elder in the Presbyterian Church for many years. Elizabeth was born August 17, 1789. He died April 3, 1874 and she died February 16, 1872. His will is recorded in Rogersville, Hawkins County, Tennessee. He bought his homesite in 1809. Some of his descendants still occupy the old homestead. (According to the 1922 writing.) Joseph was pensioned by the United States Government. Elizabeth is believed to be related to Lewis Weitzel, the celebrated Indian fighter of Virginia.

Children of Joseph Huffmaster and Elizabeth Huffmaster nee Weitzel Sarah, born Oct. 12, 1809, Married James M. Hord.

James Weitzel, Born April 26, 1811, married Mrs. Sarah Herrington Cottle.

Samuel Louderback, born April 12, 1813, Married Elizabeth A. Counts.

John, born July 26 1815 married Janes James.

Mary Ann, born July 26, 1815 married William Jones.

Lucinda, Born April 2, 1818 married Levi Campbell.

Richard Mitchell, born April 23, 1820 Married Mary F. Shanks--Twin to Richard Mitchell died at birth

Eliza Jane, born February 21. 1828, Married Abijah Anderson, February 1859; died 1860.

*Joseph, born Jan. 15, 1825, married first, Virginia Tate, October 1857; she died soon. Second, Nannie B. Huddleston.

Catherine, born 1827; died unmarried Dec. 25, 1903.

Margaret Susan, born Nov. 19, 1829; died unmarried, October 20, 1920

Lavinia Walker, born Nov. 16, 1832, Married John W. Philips

Politicians seem to run in the family. See Jos. Huffmaster (below) who sat as Juror in the case of Obediah Gents, found guilting of horse stealing. **He is Great-grand Father of Hal Harlan Huffmaster.**

The following was taken from the court records of Rogersville, Tennessee:

State Horse Stealing Vs Whereupon came a Jury to wit, 1. Hugh G. Moore, Obediah Gents 2. Henry Burim, 3. Peter Lawson, 4. John Tred-way, 5. John Ellis, 6. John Lucas, 7. Absolam Looney, 8. Jos. Huffmaster, 9. Samuel Spears, 10. Reuben Barnard, 11. Andrew Ingram, 12. Davis Howell, who being elected tried & Sworn well & truly to try & true deliverance make between the people of this and the prisoner at the Barr Obediah Gents whom the Gentry have in charge and a true verdict give according to their evidence do say the defendant is guilty in manner & form as he Stands charged in the Bill of Indictment and the Said Obediah by Samuel Powel his attorney with leave of the court enters a rule to Show cause why a new trial should be *granted.*

Authors Comment: In my research I find the information that much of what was reported in the 1922 writing is incomplete and possibly incorrect. . In that writing there is no mention of an A. D. Huffmaster, yet in the service records of the Civil War under the name of A.D. Huffmaster. The Civil War as found:

*The History Place - U.S. Civil War 1861-1865 A.D. Huffmaster, son of Joseph Huffmaster and Nannie B. Huddleston.was born Nov. 24, 2848, married Laura Lynch; no children., was inducted November 5, 1861, and was pensioned for his Civil War service. The last known survivor of the regiment was Alvin Devall Huffmaster, Pvt. , Co. E, 92, last Civil War veteran residing in Hawkins County, a retired lawyer and former mayor of Rogersville, Tennessee who died July 6, 1940.

Huffmaster, Joseph 1835 Private 59.1 Commissioner of a court house in the town of Rogersville recorded pension as follows: NAME: Huffmaster, A.D. PENSION #:S16479 UNIT: 43rd

Infantry. Information taken from United States Military Records. 2002.

*Joseph Huffmaster Tenn., Called into service at Rogersville, Hawkins County, Tenn., November 5, 1861. Known as the "Mount Sterling Banner Boys"

The following Excerpt is taken from the record of the:
Forty-third Regiment Tennessee Volunteers
(Gillespie's Infantry)
Confederate States Army
also known as
5th East Tennessee Volunteer Regiment
and later as,
43rd Tennessee Regiment Cavalry

FOURTH GENERATION

Richard Mitchell Huffmaster, Married Mary F. Shanks, June 29, 1842. She was the daughter of David M. and Elizabeth Shanks. They moved To Springdale, Arkansas following the Civil War. Their children were all born in Rogersville, Tenn., where he and all his father's children were born. Richard Mitchell was an estimable citizen. He served as Mayor of Springdale; was a justice of the peace; an elder in the Presbyterian Church and an Odd Fellow. He died Feb. 23, 1899. Mary was born May 22, 1824 and died July 9, 1865.

Children of Richard Mitchell Huffmaster and Mary F. Shanks

Elizabeth Catherine, born April 5, 1843, married her cousin J. Thomas Huffmaster. *J. Thomas Huffmaster was the son of John Huffmaster. John Huffmaster was the son of Joseph Huffmaster and Elizabeth Weitzel.* J. Thomas died Jan. 8, 1914 and Elizabeth Catherine died Dec. 23, 1913

Mary Frances, born November 30, 1844, died October 27 1897

Annis Adelia, born Oct. 7, 1846 Married first B. F. Overton; second, John A. Nelson, April 14, 1887. They had no children.

Sally Hord, born April 23, 1848, Married B. W. Cavness March 6, 1900. They had no children.

Hugh Walker Born March 3, 1850

Martha Lavinia, born December 5, 1851, died February 21, 1852.

Margaret Eliza, born Feb. 21, 1853, married Calvin Holcomb.

Ida Ann, born Dec. 20, 1854.

<u>John Martin, born Dec. 1, 1856; married Lydia W. Pearson.</u>

John Martin was my grandfather. Lydia Warren Pearson was born April 16, 1860 and died July 3, 1937 at Elm Springs, Washington County, Arkansas USA.

Parents of Lydia Warren were Jeremiah Pearson 1831-1865 and Sultana Barrington 1839-1911. Married John Martin Huffmaster in 1880.

FIFTH GENERATION

John Martin Huffmaster:

He was born Dec. 1, 1856; married Lydia W. Pearson, Sept. 15, 1880; born April 16, 1860.

Children of John Martin Huffmaster and Lydia W. Pearson:

Maude Elizabeth, born Aug. 27, 1881; died Oct. 3, 1882

Hugh Watson, born April 15, 1883; died Oct. 30 1884.

<u>Hal Harland born June 12, 1885 (my father); married Rettie George</u>, July 7, 1906.

Ida Sultana, born Aug. 29, 1887; married Perry Norman; Nov. 14, 1912

Sarah Kate, born Nov. 9, 1889; married Arthur Clede Fogle.

Mary Mitchell, born March 11, 1892; married Charles N. Havens.

Lydia Rebecca, born Sept. 29, 1894; married John Brown, July 2 1920.

Joseph Martin, born March 29, 1897; married Lela

Pebble Lavinia, born April 5, 1902; married

Margaret Adelia, born Sept. 21, 1904; married.

John Martin was our grandfather. He built and lived in a log house in Washington County, Arkansas. He was a dirt farmer who owned about 75 acres of land. Much of the land was forest. I can remember a small orchard which contained apples, peaches and grapes. He also raised bees. The bee hives were along a lane that was the egress to the house. While some of the above members of the family and their children were visiting, they found the lane was a good place to run and play tag. I was the youngest and of course the smallest and was always the tag-a-long. One day while playing the bees swarmed. I was stung several times.

Grandpa was really upset. He picked me up and pulled the bees from my long hair out with his bare hands. I really don't remember any more about Grandpa except that he had a white beard, mustache and hair. He was a very kind old man.

Don't really remember my Grandmother. She was always in her kitchen into which I was not allowed. I do remember her hat pin. She always told me when we were in the car going to church that if I didn't behave she was going to stick me with it. I have a child's memory of a long pin with a black head coming at me.

SIXTH GENERATION

Hal Harland Huffmaster married Rettie George, July 8, 1906; born Sept. 2, 1886 in Fort Worth Texas.

24

She traveled with her parents by covered wagon when 6 months old to Elm Springs, Arkansas.

They celebrated their Golden Wedding Anniversary July 8, 1956 with over 100 family and friends.

Hal died February 1, 1963 at the Springdale Memorial Hospital and is buried in Elm Springs Cemetery, Elm Springs, Washington County, Arkansas. Rettie died October 3, 1973 at the home of son, John William in Carthage, Missouri. They were both members of the Cave Springs Baptist Church, Cave Springs, Arkansas where their funeral services were held. They both were buried in the Elm Springs Cemetery, Elm Springs, Washington County, Arkansas.

Memorial written by Pastor J.N. Parish, of Cave Springs Baptist Church.

This beautiful memorial is made from blue-grey granite and stands out from the ordinary because of the outstanding design and ornamentation. It is polished both front and back and has a graceful serpentine top. The family name is carved on a contrasting panel with a cultured rose in each corner. The rose is symbolic of love and family devotion.

The names are carved on open books which symbolizes the Word of God and the scroll with the marriage date connecting the two panels makes it particularly well-suited for a companion monument.

The epitaph at the bottom of the panels "Gone But Not Forgetten" is carved on a contrasting panel.

The family name on the polished back is surrounded by the roses making it a stately memorial in the cemetery. This is truly a beautiful memorial and one that will stand forever for all to see…a symbol of the love that was shared in their life together.

Children of Hal Harland Huffmaster and Rettie George

John William, born May 8, 1907, died Dec. 3, 1980, Joplin Missouri; married Georginia Downman, 1930 She died: he married Mable Ann Ford, May 16, 1969 in Carthage, Missouri.

Sarah Lydia Mabel, born Aug. 80, 1909;

Lelia Opal, born Jan 2, 1912

Helen Ruby, born March 13, 1914;

Martin Harland, born June 12, 1916,

Jessie Barnett,JB; born Dec. 8, 1919;

Rettie Virginia, born April 27, 1928;

SEVENTH GENERATION

John William, (Bill) was born May 8, 1907 Died December 3, 1980 in Joplin, Missouri. He married Georginia Downam in 1920. They were the parents of 6 children before her death..

His second wife, Mable Ann Ford, May 16, 1969 in Carthage, Missouri. She had 2 daughters by a previous marriage. Bill was a self taught automobile mechanic. After he married Mable Ann Ford he purchased and operated a "filling station" in Carthage, Missouri until his death.

Children of John William and Georgia:

Norma Lee, Deceased;

Lonnie;

Retta Mae;

Francis

Darrell

Billy is Pastor of Baptist church in Mississippi

Children of Sarah and Allen: Kaleb April 26, 2000.

Further relations of Jimmy & Geraldine are:

Jerry, married Susan Looney, 1 child Toney married Linda Winters 1 child Luke, born January 10, 1982.

Judy married Iris Shepherd August 14, 1987, 1 child, Natasla, born December 19, 1991.

Ricky married Cathy Holt, March 8, 1980.

Children of Ricky and Cathy are: Brandon, born December 20, 1981

Sarah Lydia Mabel , born Aug. 8, 1909; died July 9, 1991, married Louis Burton, died, November 27, 1962.

Children of Sarah Lydia Mabel and Louis Burton:

Bettie Louise, married Mallard, died August 17, 2007.

Harlan, deceased: April 20, 1997, rests in Elm Springs cemetery. He married Barbara Blakemore.

Jimmy married Geraldine Reynolds, November 12, 1953, Children of Jimmy and Geraldine are:

Brenda marriedNorman Traxler, December 26, 1971; Children: Timothy, born September 26, 1974 married Gini Agnew, March 13, 1990. Their children:

Mitchell, born September 24, 1990, Ansrew, Born January 20, 1999 and Adrian, Born February 27, 2001. Sarah, daughter of Brenda and Norman, born September 28, 1977. She married Allen Grubbs, September 26, 1997. Children: Kaleb, born Arpil 26, 2000.

Further relations of Jimmy and Geraldine are: Jerry, married Susan Looney, 1 child, Toney married Linda Winters, 1 child Luke, born January 10, 1982

Judy married Iris Shepherd, August 14, 1987, 1 child, Natasla, born December 19, 1991.

Ricky married Cathy Holt, March 8, 1980. Children: Brandon, born December 20, 1981, Richard, Born July 10, 1984 and Tyler, born August 2, 1988.

Dwayne married Leann Hall, June 24, 1984. Shildren: Ashley, Born July 18, 1986, Christal, born March 8, 1988, Mariah, born August 2, 1995.

The last child of Mabel and Louis was Kathryn, born January 24, 1940 married Kenneth Wright, August 15, 1956. He died February 18, 1984. Kathryn's twin, Mary died at birth.

Lilia Opal Byrd nee Huffmaster

Lelia Opal Byrd was born January 2, 1912. She married Sterling Byrd born April 12, 1900 in Washington County Arkansas. Lelia died: November 8, 2005 at Fayetteville Arkansas. Sterling died: September 1, 1984 in Fayetteville, Arkansas. Their daughter, CoEtta Elizabeth Glasco nee Byrd was born January 22, 1939, married Michael Lowell Glasco December 27, 1969 in Dallas, Texas. They currently live in Fairview, Texas.

Helen Ruby Huffmaster, born March 13, 1914 in Elm Springs, Washington County, AR Died Dec. 20, 1995 In Bowie, Prince George's county, Maryland. Married Arthur Donald Burton, Dec. 12, 1931 in Elm Springs, AR

Arthur Donald was born April 11, 1910 in Arkansas City, Cowley Co. Kansas and died Dec. 11, 1991 in Pittsburg, Crawford. Co. Kansas. Both are buried in the Garden of Memories Cemetery, Pittsburg, Kansas in the Masonic Section Helen Ruby Huffmaster, born March 13, 1914 in Elm Springs, Washington Co. AR Died Dec. 20, 1995 In Bowie, Prince George's county, Maryland. Married Arthur Donald Burton, Dec. 12, 1931 in Elm Springs, AR

Arthur Donald was born April 11, 1910 in Arkansas City, Cowley Co.

Kansas and died Dec. 11, 1991 in Pittsburg, Crawford. Co. Kansas. Both are buried in the Garden of

Memories Cemetery, Pittsburg, Kansas in the Masonic Section

Children of Ruby and Arthur Burton

1.Catherine Laverne Burton, born Aug. 2, 1932 Elm Springs, AR at home. Died Aug 2, 1932 in Elm Springs. Buried in Elm Springs Cemetery, Elm Springs, AR

2.Helen Elizabeth Burton, born March 13, 1934, Kingston, AR at home. Married Richard James Whitaker, Sept. 11, 1955 in Pittsburg, Kansas. He was born Oct. 29, 1933 in Olathe, Johnson Co. Kansas

Children of Helen and Dick Whitaker:

1.David Craig Whitaker, born June 3, 1959 in Great Bend, Barton co. Kansas. Married Nancy Lee Byrum

Helen Married James Earlwood Henderson, June 13, 1981 in Bowie Maryland. He was born Feb. 23, 1929 in Waynesburg, Greene co. PA at home. July 29 in Mt. Rainier, Prince George's co., Maryland. Married Laurie Ann Early, about 1992 in Huntingtown, MD.

Children of David and Nancy are 1. Michael Craig Whitaker, born Oct. 26, 1980, Cheverly, Maryland 2. Robyn Lee Whitaker, born Nov. 21, 1985,

Cheverly, MD. 3. Nicholas James Whitaker, born Aug. 26, 1987, Cheverly, Maryland.

Michael Craig married Leanne Nicole Anderson, June 19, 2006 in Odenton, Maryland. Their children are 1. Kylie Jade Whitaker, born about 2004, and 2. Shawn Michael, born in 2007.

2. Patricia Ann Whitaker, born Oct. 10, 1967 in Cheverly, Prince George's co. Maryland. Married David Fugitt 1987 in Mt. Rainier, Md.

Married Ronald Raymond Schultz about 1991.

Patricia Ann and David Fugitt had one son, born

May 19, 1988 in Silver Spring, Maryland, and died Sept 14, 1988. Buried in Ft. Lincoln Cemetary, Bladensburg, Maryland

Children with Ron Schultz are Catherine Elizabeth Schultz, born Sept.

9, 1994 in Waldorf, Charles county,Maryland and Sean Whitaker Schultz, born Sept. 25. 1996 in Waldorf, Maryland.

3. Bruce Arthur Burton, born Oct. 1, 1935, Kingston AR at home. He married Betty Lou Mason, June 1955 in Cherokee, Crawford co. Kansas

Children of Bruce Burton and Betty Mason:
Cheryl Lynn Burton
Gayle Sue Burton
Brenda Kay Burton
Terri Leigh Burton.

Martin Harland, born June 12, 1916, married Ola Mae Neal, May 30, 1935 at Elm Springs, Arkansas. date of death (martin) Ola Mae still living in NW Arkansas.

Martin was a farmer at Centerton, Arkansas. He

planted and harvested many acres of wheat and oats during the growing season. In addition, he had a dairy farm where he raised chickens. He also grew a big garden and killed and sugar cured hogs to feed his family. He later worked at Kraft Foods in Bentonville, Arkansas.

Children of Martin and Ola Mae:

Billy Wayne born September 13, 1937. He married Gail Collins in 1955. No children. Second marriage was to Lavanda (Bonnie) Brown and they had 2 children, Thonda Sherlene and Regina Michelle. Third marriage was to Juanita Emmitt. They had 2 children, Oleta Racene (died at birth) and Romona Kay. They adopted Carla Faye Emmitt.

Wayne loved the farm as he grew up in Centerton, Arkansas with his dad and mom. He had several head of Holstine cattle until he married. After he married he moved to Galup New Mexico where he was a train switchman. He had several residences before moving back to Arkansas; a truck driver in Monett, Missouri then back to Russelville, Arkansas. It was there he died of cancer at age 44.

Winifred Eugene born December 10, 1929. He married Shirley Bowen. They had a son, Douglas Gregory. His second marriage was to Maxine Taylor. They had 2 children, Scotty Eugene and Ola Susan.

He left home at age 16, moved to Springdale, Arkansas to live with his Grandma and Grandpa Neal. He became a truck driver, moved to Gravette, Arkansas to manage a truck terminal for Jones Truck Lines. Later Jones moved him to Russellville to another terminal. Jones Truck line was sold when Charlie Jones died. There after, Winiford drove for other company's until he retired in 2002.

Bobby Norris born November 17, 1942. He married Carolyn Sue Brown in 1959. They had 4 children, Zebby Lynn, Bobby Glen, Judy Lanette and Ronald Lee.

With experience, he became the owner and operator of Huffmaster Trucking in Missouri.

Velva Darlene was born June 9, 1945. She married Cleburn Alvin Cline June 26, 1963, They had 2 children. Tim Alvin and Tammy Darlene. Darlene loved the farm where she grew up. She moved to the city when she and Cleburn married. Her first job was at Tyson's Egg Plant, Springdale, Arkansas. Following that she was a st-at-home mom taking care of the 2 children until they started school. She then went back to school to earn her degree in accounting. After graduation she worked in accounting at Emerson Electric until it shut down. She currently works at Wal-Mart, Rogers, Arkansas in the accounting department.

Martin Floyd was born in 1947. He married Linda Kay Breadlove and they had 3 children, Aaron Harlin, Billy Joe Brian and Elizabeth Jeanette. His second marriage was to Pat. They had no children.

He was a truck driver while growing up in Centerton, Arkansas. He served in the Viet Nam conflict/Army/ He came home safely, built his own boat and returned to truck driving in Salasaw, Oklahoma.

Ivan Glen was born January 14, 1951. He married Dianne Samples. They had 3 children, Angela Marie, Tabatha Jean and Ivan Glen. Ivan grew up in Centerton, Arkansas. Started truck driving at a very young age. Following his year of driving for someone else hauling chickens rather than moving them, he started raising them and also ran his own barbecue catering business.

Linda Maxine was born June 15, 1953. She married Dan Allen Sams. He passed away in March 2000. They had 2 natural born children and 3 adopted. Natural born: Danny Eugene and Robert Allen. Those adopted were: Rebecca Mae Sams, Jessica Rae Sams and Michael Brandon.

Linda married Wes Martindale. She always loved singing, playing piano and having family get-togethers. She was born when Martin and Ola Mae lived on the Centerton farm. They moved to Springdale, Arkansas when she was very young. Having studied in the medical field, she went to work at Springdale Hospital as a nurse assistant while she was still in school. After graduation she went into nursing as a licensed tjem a Registered Nurse in recovery. She later received her Registration and worked part time at Washington Regional Hospital on the I.V. team. She currently work in recovery at Bates Hospital, Bentonville, Arkansas.

Danny Joe was born February 14, 1955 mentally challenged. He has never been able to talk. Martin and Ola Mae kept him at home until it was no longer possible. He, then was placed in the Arkansas Children's Colony, Conway, Arkansas. Danny Joe still resides at the Colony.

Jessie Barnett, born December 8, 1919 (July 4, 1997), married Francille Haynes, April 21, 1939 (April, 1998). (Need place and dates of their death and where they are buried.

Jessie (JB) left home in Elm Springs, Arkansas to attend a Baptist College in Magnolia, Arkansas. After, he attended the Baptist College, Marshall, Texas while holding a pastoral position in Atlanta, Texas. He served churches in Pastoral positions including Arkansas, Texas, Louisiana then back to Arkansas.

He retired, because of ill health, and with the help of his sons, built a home near Waldo, Arkansas. On that property, they dug a pond and seeded it with catfish. Only one problem existed, it became infested with water moccasins.

JB and Francille were the parents of 5 children.

Sarah, Stillborn

JB, Jr **Sara Rae Huffmaster** (Great Granddaughter of Jessie Barnett Huffmaster)

Jason and Heather Huffmaster of Paragould have announced the birth of a daughter on April 18, 2007, at St. Bernards in Jonesboro. The baby weighed eight pounds, six ounces, and has been named Sara Rae Huffmaster.

She has a brother, Jacob Huffmaster, who is four.

Grandparents are Diane Moore and Vernon Moore, both of Hoxie, and J.B. and Jeanette Huffmaster of Paragould. She is the great-granddaughter of David and Bertha Huckabay of Paragould, Ray and Elsie Clark of Black Rock and Della Moore of Hoxie.

Richard
Fred
Debbie

Richard B. Huffmaster, born January 31, 1946 married Betty C. Ermert, born July 28, 1948 in September 1970.

He attended Louisiana Tech University in Ruston, Louisiana and graduated in 1973. He was employed by the Federal Land Bank, a lending agency to farmers and worked for them for 19 years. Currently Rick is employed by the Army Corps of Engineers in Little Rock, Arkansas as a real estate appraiser and has worked there for the past 17 years. Betty attended Arkansas State University and graduated from there in 1970. She received a teacher's degree from Louisiana College in Alexandria, Lousiana. She is retired and Rick plans to retire in 2010. Prior to his employment, Rick was a member of the US armed services for 4 years as an Aircraft Mechanic in the Air Force following his training in Texas. He was stationed in Viet Name and finally at England Air Force Base in Alexandria, Louisiana.

Richard and Betty are the parents of 2 sons.

Robert Andrew, born July 21, 1974 and married

Jody Caldwell, April 29, 2000. They have 2 children Hattie Claire, 3 years old and Benjamin Barnett, 2 years old.

William Blake born September 26, 1980 and married Andera Phillips on Mar 19, 2006. They have 1 son, Hayden Ryan, 7 months old.

Rettie Virginia, born April 27, 1928; married Thomas Gregory Farrell, June 25, 1965, St. Mary of Celle Church, Berwyn, Illinois.

Thomas died February 20, 1980, rests in Resurrection Cemetery, Justice, Illinois.

They lived in an apartment in Berwyn, Illinois when first married. Their first child was born there. When the second child was born, they moved to LaGrange Park, Illinois to a larger apartment.

Their move to Willow Springs, Illinois was when the third child was on the way. They purchased the home, where Virginia still lives and added 2 more children to the list, making a full house

Children of Tom & Virginia Farrell nee Huffmaster are:

Barbara Elaine, born March 28, 1966, at MacNeal Hospital, Berwyn, Illinois. She married John Truby, born July 28, 1955 in Chicago, Illinois. They have 2 daughters, Veronica, born October 17, 1990, Kathleen Margaret, born November 4, 1994. Barbara is a teacher at Noterdam School for Boys in Forest Park. Barbara and John reside in Chicago.

Virginia Louise, born March 17, 1967, at MacNeal Hospital, Berwyn, Illinois. She married Will Gentleman, born date, have 5 daughters, divorced. She lives in Wheeling, Illinois. He lives in Mokena, Illinois.

Fabian Gregory, born November 2, 1959, married Eileen Boldyga, March , 1982, Eileen was born, have 2 daughters: Kelli Marie and Sara. They live in Pleasant Prairie, Wisconsin.

Stephen Michael, born July 31, 1961. Lives in Park Ridge, Illinois. Not married.

Theresa Marie, born April 15, 1967, married Ronald Hathaway, February 20, at Episcopal Church, Mokena, Illinois, have 2 daughters: Melanie Ann and Jennifer Marie and 1 son, Thomas Randolph. They live in New Lenox, Illinois.

LAUTERBACH RECORDS
Burgess's Tx-Mo
Updated: April 18, 2002

1. *Anna Margrethe* FEY was born about 1661 IN Germany. She married *Johann Niklaus LAUTERBACH* about 1680 in Germany. He was born about 1660 in Germany.

Child of Anna Margrethe FEY and Johann Niklaus Lauterbach **is:**

+2 I. *Johannes Ludwig Lauterbach* was born 1652 in Staudernheim,   Germany and died May 16, 1736 in Studernheim, Germany.

From Ancestry World Tree: Burgess's Tx-Mo April 18, 2002-sherri schappert

Descendant Register, Generation No. 1

Descendant Register, Generation No. 2

2. Johannes Ludwig Lauterbach (Anna Margrethe FEY) was born 1652 in Staudernheim, Germany and died May 16, 1736 in Staudernheim, Germany.   He was buried May 16, 1736. He married Anna Margrethe Gratzman, January 12 1705/06 in Staudernheim. She was born March 27, 1680 In Staudernheim, Germany and died February 1745/46 in Staudernheim, Germany. She was buried February 27. 1745/46 in Staudernheim, Germany.

Children of Johannes Ludwig Lauterbach and Anna Margrethe Gratzmann:

Maria Katharina Christened December 4, 1712 in Staudernheim, Germany. She married Johann Nikolaus Holzapiel, Son of Johann Martin Halzapfel

Johannes Lautenbach Christened February 17, 1723/24 in Staudernheim, Germany

Johan David Lauterbach who was christened January 25, 1716/17 in Frankfurt, Hessen, N. Prussia. Johan David Lauterbach died 1793 in Shenandoah, Virginia.

Descendant Register, Generation No. 3

Johan David Lauterbach married Maria Elizabetha Klein July 15, 1745 in Lititz, Lancaster, Pennsylvania. She was born about 1724 in Of, Virginia.

Children of Johan David Lauterbach and Maria Elizabetha Klein are:

David Louderback, born 1746 In Lancaster County, Pennsylvania, died AFT. 1810 in Hawkins, Tennessee.

Christine Lauderback born July 16, 1746 in Virginia and died March 12, 1825 in Gap Mills, Monroe, Virginia

John Louderback, born 1749 in Frederick County, Virginia. He married Eve.

Matthias Louderback was born 1749 in Frederick County, Virginia and died 1807 in Shenandoah, Virginia.

Susannah Louderback, born 1750 in Virginia. Married Ernest Frederick about 1780 in Virginia.

Joseph Louderback was born 1751 in Virginia and died 1828 in Shenandoah, Virginia. Daniel Louderback, born 1753 in Virginia, he married Anne Ward, July 27, 1790 in Virginia.

Abraham Louderback, born 1755 in Virginia, married Margaret Comer in 1786 in Virginia. Margaret was the daughter of Adam Comer and Margaret. She was born about 1755 in VirginiBarbara Louderback was born 1761 in Virginia. She married Peter Henry Helvey, July 22, 1792 in Virginia.

<u>Sarah Louderback was born 1764 in Frederick, Virginia</u>.

Eve Louderback was born 1770 in Frederick, Virginia. She married Abraham Campbell in 1799 in Virginia.

Elizabeth Louderback was born 1772 In Frederick, Virginia. She married John Burdidge.

Descendant Register, Generation No. 4

At this point is the separation of the Lauterbach family and the joining of the Huffmaster family.

Sarah Louder back (Johan David Lauterbach, Johannes

Ludwig Lauterbach, Anna Margrethe Fey) was born 1764 in Frederick, Virginia. She married Gottlieb Huffmaster, June 12, 1781 in Virginia. He was born about 1757 in Germany and died about 1844 in Hawkins, Tennessee

Children of Sarah Lauderback and Gottlieb Huffmaster are: Joseph Huffmaster born April 4, 1782 In Shenandoah, Virginia and died AFT.

1870 In Hawkins, Tennessee. In addition there was a son, Godlove Huffmaster born June 11, 1798 in Shenandoah, Virginia.

This information seems to disclaim that of James Huffmaster and his opinion that Gottlieb Huffmaster changed his name to Godlove Huffmaster. (from James Huffmaster's Huffmaster/Hoffmeister: " Gottlieb Hoffmeister arrived in America about 1776, and settled in Shenandoah County, Virginia. He was born about 1757, in the vicinity of Frankfort on the Main in Germany. He changed the spelling of his name to Godlove Huffmaster;) Actually, Godlove Huffmaster was the son of Gottlieb Hoffmeister and it is possible that Gottlieb's middle name was Godlove. It does seem likely that Godlove was struck and killed by lightning as James Huffmaster said.

George Family History

William Andrew George, born August 16, 1857 in Fort Worth, Tarrant County, Texas. Died, February 8, 1927 in Elm Springs, Washington County, Arkansas.

He married Sarah Jane Sexton, November 1876 in Brown County, Indiana. Sarah Jane was born Mark 8 1858, died March 23, 1931 in Elm Springs, Washington County Arkansas. They were buried in Elm Springs Cemetery, Elm Springs, Washington County, Arkansas.

Parents of William Andrew George were James Enoch George and Margaret Stogsdill. Parents of Sarah Jane Sexton were David S. Sexton and William Anna Rogers.

The children of William Andrew George and Sarah Jane Sexton George were:

Guildy George, born December 23, 1877 in Fort Worth, Tarrant County, Texas. She died October 22, 1890

Mary Jane George, born March 8, 1880 in Fort Worth, Tarrant County, Texas

Died, August 29, 1905 in childbirth in Johonson, Washington County, Arkansas, buried August 31, 1905 In Johnson Cemetery, Washington County, Arkansas .

James David George, born July 3, 1884 in Fort

Worth, Tarant County, Texas. He died November 29, 1883

Martin Arnold George, Born March 31, 1895 at Elm Springs, Washington County, Arkansas. Died February 1970 at Springdale, Washington County, Arkansas, buried in Elm Springs Cemetery, Elm Springs, Washington County, Arkansas

Rettie George, Born September 2, 1886 at Tarrant County, Texas. Died October 3, 1973 at Carthage, Missouri, buried in Elm Springs Cemetery, Washington County, Arkansas.

Charles Lee George, born December 29, 1888 at Elm Springs, Washington County, Arkansas. He died May 26, 1969 at Springdale, Washington County, Arkansas. He is buried in Bluff Cemetery, Washington County, Springdale, Arkansas.

Artie George, born about 1890. (No other record can be found

Oatie May George, born August 1890 at Elm Springs, Washington County, Arkansas, died January 1, 1961 in Arkansas City, Cowley County, Kansas. She is buried in Arkansas City, Cowley County, Kansas.

Elde George, born about 1892. (No other record can be found.(same as Artie)

William Enoch George, Born November 1892 at Elm Springs, Washington County, Arkansas. He died January 28, 1973 in Elm Springs, Washington County, Arkansas, buried in Bluff Cemetery, Washington County, Arkansas.

9. Henry Lewis George, born December 2 1897 at Elm Springs, Washington County, Arkansas, died May 26, 1939, Elm Springs, Washington County Arkansas.

He is buried in Elm Springs Cemetery, Elm Springs, Washington County, Arkansas.

January 9, 1974, the following article written by Euna Belle George Allen (daughter of Henry George and Flora George) appeared in the Pea Ridge Arkansas Newspaper. The article had a graphic of the William A. George Family.

George Family Settled Near Elm Springs *Flora*

By Edna Belle George Allen

The William George family settled in Northwest Arkansas in the late 1890's. Originally from Indiana, going to Texas and then back to Arkansas by covered wagon, they homesteaded a farm on the ridge, west of Elm Springs.

Mr. George was a fruit farmer planting his own orchards labor building his own evaporator where apples were peeled, sliced and dried with furnaces. The fruit was transported by wagon and team to Springdale and shipped by railroad from that area.

The family also raised their own sorghum cane and operated their own sorghum mill each fall.

Income from these occupied provided livelihood for the family of four daughters and four sons. One daughter died at the age of eleven. Another daughter, Anna, married the late Jim Loper and died bearing three small daughters. (Two of these daughters are still living and in Springdale, Mrs. Annie Morris and Mrs. Bertha Neal.) Mr. Loper later married another daughter, Nettie George.

Mr. and Mrs. George moved to Elm Springs about 1910 and lived there until their deaths. They were members of the Brush Creek Baptist Church but later moved their membership to the Baptist Church in Elm Springs located just south of the Elm Springs cemetery.

Mr. George died in 1928 and Mrs. George in 1933.

After leaving Indiana, Mrs. George never saw any of her relatives again. Her father was a Baptist preacher.

Henry George died in 1930. The other four children pictured have died within the last five years.

This story has been written by what I can remember and from some few notes and records that I have. I do know that when Grandpa George passed away in '28 that my parents moved from Oklahoma to Elm Springs to live with Grandma George. I wish I could remember the stories that she loved to tell of their experiences, when they traveled by covered wagon and their encounter with the Indians. My Grandparents had very little education but I do remember that I never noticed a dictionary when she was around because there wasn't any word that she couldn't spell.

All of this family is gone, but their posterity is scattered all over the U.S. A large number are still in the Northwest Arkansas area, and especially Springdale.

Several different services could be rendered to Grandpa today by his grandchildren if he were to appear on the scene, he could eat his meals at Neal's Cafe in Springdale and buy food for chickens, and the chickens, as well as cattle and feed supplies at George's Feed in Springdale. Jesse Morris has a pump service and Grandpa then could have his taxes figured at John Allen's Accountant office. One son and grandson of Henry George are Baptist preachers. One son and grandson of Nettie Burg are Baptist preachers. This is just to mention a few.

One memory I have is that this family was taught to work and use of their labor.

THIS PICTURE OF THE WILLIAM A. GEORGE FAMILY is shared by Edna Belle George Allen of Cave Springs, who identifies those seen as follows: First lady and small girl (unknown); William A. George; Sarah Jane (Sexton) George; Henry George (Father of Mrs. Harvey Allen); Charlie George (founder of George Poultry Industries of Springdale); back row, first lady (unknown); Martin George; William E. George; Hal Buttonster; Willis Huffmaster; (Now living in the Joplin, Mo. area); Nettie (George) Huffmaster. The picture was taken in front of their homestead. Tom Sexton. This was the birthplace of Mrs. Allen, also, Three daughters of the couple are not pictured.

The following pages contain data found on the web. This data traces the Hoffmeister Genealogy back to the 15ᵗʰ century, found via Ancestry.com, RootsWeb.com and through searches of various names on the web.

Up to the late war the courts of Germany and Austria had their official Hofmeister, a position of dignity and importance.

According to the records of the Christian Church during the reformation of Martin Luther, John Hofmeister was the Vicar General of Worms and Ratisbon, Germany. Melchior Kirchhofer (of Schaffhausen, 1773-1853) wrote a biography of John Hofmeister. Since Zurich was the place of the start of the reformation by Martin Luther, it is mentioned in the records of the Christian Church that: "Zurich was now no longer the sole centre of Reform. St Schaff-hausen, John Hoffmeister at Biel, Wyttenbach and other in different areas of Germany were preaching freely. The reformers suffered greatly at the hands of the Catholic Heirachy. There is no records, that I have been able to find, as to the death, etc. of John Hofmeister. With the comparison of dates between John and Gottlieb it leads me to believe that John may have been the great, great grandfather of Gottlieb.

===

Following are names of actual Reformers of Zofingen listed in the membership as the first new convert preacher appointed from Bern. Doctor Johann Sebastian Hofmeister, diversity predicant came to Zofinger in May 1528. He died June 26, 1533.

Included in the names of actual Reformers of Zofingen was the great reformer: Martin Luther(1483-1546.) Martin Luther protested many things the Roman Catholic Church taught following his Ordination into the Priesthood. This led to his excommunication from the Roman Church. While studying and heading the reformation drive, he married and began his preaching as a Protestant. He made great inroads especially in Zurich.

This resulted in his trial at: The Diet of Worms.

In 1512 Zurich was no longer the focal point of the reformation; it had extended to Schaff-hausen, where Johann Sebastian Hofmeister was Vicar General of Worms and was present at the Diet of worms to support Luther during his interrogation.

Excerpts from the Diet of Worms: 1512 and From: Excerpts of the History of the Christian Church Vo9lumn VIII (The History of the Reformation by Philip Schaff, third edition. http://genforum.genealogy.com/cgi-bin/ pageload.cgi?Gottlieb,Hoffmeister::hoffmeister::40.html

Articles found on line.

Various Sites of information that could be connected to the Hofmeister/Huffmaster family records.

Credit for the following is given to: Ancestry World Tree: burgess Tex-Mo

Hofmeister: said by the **Bergdorf** 1816 census (KS 659) to have been from **Bondorf, Boeblingen [Amt]. Wuerttemberg. KS** 312 said this family was from Braunschweigueber **Neu-Verbas. Ungam. (This work is in progress for verication)** The GCRA using FHL (1,055.978) has proven them to be from **Fellbach**, like the Aldinger family into which a Hofmeister married, and to have come to Bergdorf via S. Prussia, not Hungary.

There is an article that proves that there were very dignified personage in the Hofmeister family. James Huffmaster relates that Gottfried Hoffmeister was the Hoffmeister (Episcopal Œconomous) for the period in Germany prior to his traveling to the America's.. According to the Greek interpretation of an Economous he was the keeper of records.

A Hofmeister prior to
Gottfried was Augustus Hofmeister.

He was a Episcopal Economous in a Catholic Cathedral until his abdication to Christianity during the time Martin Luther wrote and published his Thesis.

Sebastian Hofmeister

Encyclopædia Britannica Article

born 1476, Schaffhausen, Switzerland

died June 26, 1533, Zofingen

By name Oeconomus Swiss religious Reformer who was a prominent figure in the debates of the early Reformation.

Hofmeister entered the Franciscan order at Schaffhausen, and he then studied for several years in Paris, where he received a doctorate in theology (1519). In 1520 he was sent as a lecturer to Zürich and later the same year to Constance. Influenced by the Swiss Protestant Reformer Huldrych Zwingli, he openly preached Reformation notions at Lucerne (1522) and was consequently expelled from the town. Returning to Schaffhausen, Hofmeister became the city's principal Reformer before he was forced to flee again (1525);

eventually he found safety in Zürich. He was active in the early Reformation debates: the first Zürich disputation (January 29, 1523); the second Zürich disputation (October 26–28, 1523), over which he initially presided; and the disputation of Bern (January 1528). He participated in the Anabaptist (Reformers advocating adult baptism) colloquies at Zürich and supervised the recantation of the Anabaptist leader Hans Pfistermeyer at Bern (April 19, 1531). He also preached in Sankt Gall and Basel, corresponded with Martin Luther, and wrote several minor works, including an autobiography.

===

Family Memories of Author
Rettie V. Farrell nee Huffmaster

John William, the oldest of the Hal and Rettie clan was always called Willie or Bill. Bill married before the author was born. His first child, Noralea was born April 20, 1926, just 2 years and seven days before this author. She died of cancer as did her mother. Following their marriage, Bill and Georgia bought a farm where they lived until she died. They parented seven children. Bill was a self-taught auto mechanic. Of course in those days, the autos were not computerized as they are today so, it was said, that Bill could listen to a Model T Ford or a Model A Ford or any other make in those days and determine the problem. Those autos, one of which belonged to our father, are now in many museums across the US. After Georgia's death, Bill bought what was called a Filling

Station and General store in Carthage, Missouri. He re-married, his second wife preceded him in death.

===

The second child of Hal and Rettie was Sarah Lydia Mabel. As I recall, Mabel and Lewis, whom she married about 1931 lived in a farm home just west of our parents in Elm Springs. They lived there until the last of the 5 children were born. Lewis worked for the Jones Trucking company in Springdale, Arkansas until his death. Mabel was an excellent cook and in her years as a widow became Chef at the University of Arkansas, Fayetteville, Arkansas. Until this day, I remember the many excellent baked beans she made.

===

Third was Lelia Opal. She had very dark eyes and black hair. Her height reached about 5 feet 5 inches. Prior to her marriage to Sterling, she was a Practical Nurse in a doctor's office in Springdale. She remained there until she and Sterling moved to Fayetteville, Arkansas. Sterling was a barber and practiced until his legs would no longer allow him to stand long periods of time. They were antique collectors and had many beautiful pieces of furniture, lamps, glass ware and rugs. Lelia had a excellent touch with the needle, making quilts and her own clothing. I recall a crib quilt she made for her daughter, Liz. It was 2 inch red and white squares. She also covered the bassinet with white eyelet embroidery fabric and trimmed it in red. For many years, she worked at a ladies clothing store as a seamstress. She was an Eastern Star. Sterling was an Odd Fellow/Mason.

===

Helen Ruby, the fourth child of Hal and Rettie married Arthur Burton. They had 3 children, the first of which was still born. Ruby and Art lived in Elm Springs, Arkansas then with his parents at Kingston, Arkansas. Art was a train man and worked for the Kansas City Southern Railroad which led them to move to Colorado. After Colorado, they settled and bought a home in Pittsburg, Kansas. Ruby was a seamstress who did alterations at a general store in Pittsburg. Ruby was Eastern Star and Arthur was an Odd Fellow. In the summer, their garden was always filled with fresh vegetables. Ruby, either canned or froze much of what was raised. In addition, they had a grape arbor. There was always, in season, a bountiful crop of grapes.

===

Martin Harland, the second boy and the fifth child of Hal and Rettie was married to Ola Mae Neal. They had 8 children. Martin was a farmer and spent most of his life at a farm in Centerton, Arkansas. Later, he and Ola Mae moved to Springdale, Arkansas. He worked for Tyson Foods as a truck driver who delivered food to chicken farmers. They were member of the Baptist Church in Springdale where Martin sang in the choir.

===

J. B. (Jessie Barnett) the sixth child of Hal and Rettie, at 17 years of age left home to attend the Southern Baptist College in Magnolia, Arkansas. While student preaching, he was sent to a church in Waldo, Arkansas. There he met Francille. They married, had 4 children and saw much of the south through his ministry. He pastured churches in Lousiana, Arkansas and Texas. While in Atlanta, Texas he attended the Baptist College in Marshall, Texas. It was there he received his MA in Christian Theology. His last assignment was in Waldo, Francille's home church.

From there he retired to a small farm. He and his sons built a home, dug a pond and stocked it with catfish. That created a problem. The pond also was for the watering of the cows he owned. They were, cows and humans, careful to stay in the cleared side of the pond as on the far side where there was vegetation there were Water Moccasins. My last visit there was just prior to his death.

==

Rettie Virginia Farrell nee Huffmaster the seventh child of Hal and Rettie was born 8 ½ years following JB. Their home was one-quarter of a mile from the old log home place settled by John Martin Huffmaster and Lydia Warren Pearson (the authors grandparents) The home where I lived sat on a hill, between 2 dry water branches. Many times one of the bridges would wash out. The county hired my dad to put up signs and call the county seat to report the problem. Most of their home was surrounded by wooded acreage; oak, maple, dog wood and elm trees. I was born just prior to the great depression and have many memories of the shortage of items. Black coal when available and was used in a free standing stove for heat. Mostly wood was used for the cook stove but when there was no black coal, wood also was used for heating during the depression years of the 1930's. When World War II broke out in 1942, the government almost immediately rationed most everything that could be bought, especially at the grocery store. We were given food stamps for each item and when those stamps were gone, they were not allowed to purchase those items until a new set of stamps was issued. Sugar and coffee were the items most everybody watched with a possessive eye. Even with the raitoning, we were not as bad off as some of our neighbors and friends who didn't raise and conserve the food supply.

Our food supply was made up of pork, which Dad and the boys butchered every fall and chicken that we raised and hens for eggs. We also had several milk cows. I was able to milk one cow (the reason for my bi-cep muscles that still linger today).

My father operated a Sorgum Mill and the molasses was used to sweeten cereal, cakes or pies. The people in the vicinity would haul wagon loads of cane to the mill where dad would cook the juice until it was syrup. At the end of the day, any children lingering around the mill, was given a molasses taffy sucker. The stick was a length of sugar cane.

No one was ever really hungry but there was little or no variety. My mother planted, raised and canned all the vegetables she could. Some of the vegetables, Irish potatoes and sweet potatoes were stored in a root cellar. In the spring, most of the potatoes had grown sprouts (eyes). They were cut up for seed planted usually on March 17, St. Patricks Day. They were harvested in the fall and that yield was also stored in the root cellar.

As the story goes: "It was a humble upbringing but: A wonderful life for a young girl with a vivid imagination."

At this writing, I am the only one left of the Hal and Rettie Huffmaster clan. Every day, I think of them and miss them. It is a lonely life, when it is impossible to talk to Mom or Dad or one of your brothers and sisters. God Bless them all!

On April 27, 2008 I reached the ripe old age of 80 years. I live alone in the home Tom and I purchased in 1959. I raise my own garden, do my own cooking, cleaning and have a Rat Terrier female dog as a companion. She will be 10 years old in September this year, 2009.

I attend church services regularly, participate in Bible Study, am a member of the adult choir and write the Church newsletter and the Epistle of Grace hard copy distributed to the congregation members every other month.

Before my senior years I was involved in local politics and filled the office of Village Clerk for 4 years and then a Trustee of the Village for 4 years. I then ran for Mayor and lost by 2 votes.

===

Whether humors or fact there are

Many interesting on-line articles that may connect the Huffmaster family to long forgotten stories. One of those is Lewis Wetzel.

Family Data Collection - Individual Records
Record about Lewis Ludwig Wetzel
Name: Lewis Ludwig Wetzel
Parents: John Wetzel , Mary Bonnett
Birth Place: Shenandoah, South Branch
Cedar Creek, VA
Birth Date: August 1763
Death Place: Adams Co, MS
Death Date: 1808
It is believed that Elizabeth Wetzel was related
to Lewis Wetzel.

It has also been said that a member of the Huffmaster family had as a ancestor an American Indian maiden spouse.. Searches have never found this to be true. There are a lot of stories about Lewis Wetzel, written by many people in the Virginia/Pennsylvania area. It remains to be learned if Lewis Wetzel was really a soldier in the Revolution or is he a legend?

Franz Anton Hoffmeister (brother of Gottfried)

was born in Rothenburg am Neckar in May 1754. When he was only 14 years old he arrived in Vienna to study law, but soon became so attracted to the city's rich musical life, that upon graduating, he decided to devote his life to music, both with composition and, as it turned out publishing. By the 1780s he had become one of the city's most popular composers, with an extensive and varied list of works to his credit. His music was geared more towards the skilled amateur market than to the professional, meaning that he was tapping into the developing middle class coming to the forefront in Vienna. **Over 15 years Hoffmeister issued works by** many prominent Viennese composers amongst them Albrechtsberger, Clementi, E.A. Förster, Ordonez, Pleyel, Vanhal and Paul Wranitzky, as well as himself. Beethoven, Mozart and Haydn are all represented in his vast catalogue, Wolfgang Amadues Mozart by several important first editions including the G minor Piano Quartet K.478, and the single String Quartet in D K.499, the 'Hoffmeister' Quartet. In 1799 Hoffmeister and the flautist Franz Thurner set off on a concert tour that was to have taken them as far a field as London. They got no further than Leipzig however, where Hoffmeister befriended the organist Ambrosius Kühnel. The two must have decided to set up a music publishing partnership for "within a year" they had founded the Bureau de Musique that would later grow into the well-respected firm of C.F. Peters, which is still active today. Until 1805 Hoffmeister kept both the Viennese firm and the newer Leipzig publishing house going, but in March 1805 he transferred sole ownership of the Bureau de Musique to Kühnel, arranging as part of the transfer a life annuity for himself.

He was a very prolific composer; popular not only in Vienna and Austria, but throughout the German states and other parts of Europe. His music can claim flowing and pleasant melodies, making them easy for amateurs to sound good with. Overall however, his style is lacking in depth and originality. For the most part, his music was out of fashion by the 1820's. Prominent in Hoffmeister's extensive listings of works are those for the flute, not only concertos but also chamber works with the flute in a leading role. Many of these works were composed with Vienna's growing number of amateur musicians in mind for whom the flute was one of the most favored instruments.

Wolfgang Amadeus Mozart
born Salzburg, 27 January 1756; died Vienna, 5 December 1791). Son of Leopold Mozart. He showed musical gifts at a very early age, composing when he was five and when he was six playing before the Bavarian elector and the Austrian empress. , In 1777 the Mozarts, seeing limited opportunity in Salzburg for a composer so hugely gifted, resolved to seek a post elsewhere for Wolfgang. He was sent, with his mother, to Munich and to Mannheim, The years 1779-80 were spent in Salzburg, playing in the cathedral and at court, composing sacred works, symphonies, concertos, serenades and dramatic music. But opera remained at the centre of his ambitions, and an opportunity came with a commission for a serious opera for Munich.

Some time during his travels is when Amadeus Mozart and Franz Hofmeister worked together. Dates of birth for both are concurrent with History.

HUFFMASTER FAMILY PICTURE -
TAKEN IN 1927

<u>Back Row Left to Right:</u>

1. Joe Huffmaster, born March 29 1879

2. John William "Willlie" Huffmaster, born May 8, 1907 (son of Hal & Rettie)

3. Euel "Don" Beard, born Oct. 27, 1900 (husband of Oma F. Brown)

4. John Brown, born January 8, 1880 (husband of Reba Huffmaster)

<u>Second Row Down Left to Right:</u>

Oma (Brown) Beard (wife of Euel "Don" Beard) holding daughter Betty Beard born about 1927

Georgia (Downum) Huffmaster (wife of Willie Huffmaster) holding daughter, Norma Lea Huffmaster, born about 1927

Lela (Aaron) Huffmaster, born June 8, 1899 (wife of Joe Huffmaster)

Lewis Burton (husband of Mabel Huffmaster)

Mabel (Huffmaster) Burton, born August 30, 1909 (daughter of Hal & Rettie)

Lelia Huffmaster, born January 2, 1912 (daughter of Hal & Rettie)

Ola Norman, born October 28, 1913 (daughter of Tannie & Perry)

Lucy Fogle, born August 2, 1914 (daughter of Kate & Clede)

Ruby Huffmaster, born March 13, 1914 (daughter of Hal & Rettie)

Lee Norman, born December 16, 1906 (son of Tannie & Perry)

Merl Fogle, born August 5, 1912 (son of Kate & Clede)

Third Row Down Left to Right:

Perry Norman, born February 13, 1868 (husband of Tannie)

Tannie (Huffmaster) Norman, born August 29, 1887

Hal Huffmaster, born June 12, 1885

Rettie (George) Huffmaster, born September 2, 1886 (wife of Hal)

Clede Fogle, born September 22, 1887 (husband of Kate)

Kate (Huffmaster) Fogle, born November 9, 1889 (wife of Clede)

Holding son John Arthur Fogle, born November 10, 1924

Pebble Huffmaster, born April 5, 1901

Ethel Norman, born March 8, 1918 (daughter of Tannie & Perry)

Wallace Norman, born November 9, 1915 (son of Tannie & Perry)

Standing in front of Wallace- Reba Norman, born February 26, 1920(daughter of Tannie & Perry)

Front Row Left to Right:

Charlie Havens, born January 5, 1895 (husband of Mary)

Sherman "Dode" Havens, born November 10, 1922

Mary (Huffmaster) Havens, born March 11, 1892

Ida Ann Huffmaster, born December 20, 1854 (sister to John Martin Huffmaster)

Sarah "Sallie" (Huffmaster) Cavness, born April 3, 1848 (sister to John Martin Huffmaster)

John Martin Huffmaster, born December 1, 1856

Lydia (Pearson) Huffmaster, born April 16, 1860

Reba (Huffmaster) Brown, born September 29, 1894 holding daughter Lillian, born January 16, 1927)

Lorene Brown, born May 29, 1921 (daughter of Reba & John Brown)

Margaret Huffmaster holding Velma Brown, born December 6, 1922 (daughter of Reba & John Brown)

Kneeling in very front Left to Right:

Martin Huffmaster, born June 12, 1916 (son of Hal & Rettie)

Margaret Fogle, born December 7, 1921 (daughter of Kate & Clede)

Ida Bell Fogle, born July 4, 1918 (daughter of Kate & Clede)

Jesse Huffmaster, born December 8, 1919 (son of Hal & Rettie)

Richard Mitchell Huffmaster   Lydia & John Martin Huffmaster

Brothers & Wives
Left: Joe and Lila Huffmaster
Right: Hal & Rettie Huffmaster

Mabel, Lelia, Ruby, Jessie, Virginia. 5 of Hal and Rettie's children about 1988

Left to right in Picture: 1. Tanny Norman, 2. Joe & Lela Huffmasterm 3. Louis Burton, 4. Mable Burton, 5. Hal Huffmaster, 6. Rettie Huffmaster, 7. Mary Havens, 8. Charles Havens, 9. Lelia Huffmaster, 10. Lydia Warren Huff master (Hal's Mother) 11. John William Huff master (Hal's Father. I believe the little boy in the front row is Jessie Huffmaster and to his with a fist on her head may be me, Virginia Huffmaster. Sorry, I can't place names with the others.

Written on back.
Grand pa Huffmaster

Perry & Tanni Norman (Hals's sister)
John Martin Huff master (Hals's Father)

OBITUARIES

Newspaper Obit--Thursday, July 11, 1940
A. D. Huffmaster, 92, confederate Veteran, dies at his
home here. He was the last of the confederate Veterans
in Hawkins County: Funeral Sunday.
(43rd TN Infantry, I Company, CSA)

A.D. Huffmaster, 92, last Civil War veteran residing
in Hawkins County, a retired lawyer and former mayor
of Rogersville, died Saturday at his home here where he
had lived nearly all his life. Mr. Huffmaster joined the
Confederate forces when a boy of 13, first serving as
messenger boy under his brother, Capt. Joe Huffmaster
whose company was stationed near Kingsport.

Mr. Huffmaster, son of Methodist minister, was born
in Newport, KY., in 1848 and came to Rogersville when
11 years old to live with an aunt. He was admitted to the
bar in 1873 and was a leader of the Hawkins County Bar
Association for more than 60 years. He was also one of
East Tennessee's leading Democrats. He retired in 1928
from his law firm because of declining health.

Hal H. Huffmaster, 77, resident of 1012 Watson, died
yesterday morning in Springdale Memorial Hospital. He

was born June 12, 1885, at Elm Springs. He was a retired farmer and a member of the First Baptist Church At Cave Springs. Survivors include his wife, Rettie of the home; three sons, Willie of Joplin, Mo. Jessie B. of Success Ark., and Martin of Springdale; four daughters, Mrs. Mable Burton of Springdale, Mrs. Lelia Byrd of Fayetteville, Mrs. Ruby Burton of Pittsburg, Kansas, and Mrs. Virginia Farrell of Willow Springs, Illinois: three sisters, Mrs. Tannie Norman of Springdale, Mrs. Margaret Harris of Springdale, and Mrs. Kate Fogle of Denver, Colorado; 30 grandchildren and 33 great-grandchildren. Funeral will be at 10 a.m. Monday in the First Baptist Church at Cave Springs. Burial will be in the Elm Springs Cemetery under the direction of Callison-Sisco Funeral Home.

February 1, 1963   Just Sleeping
Now the laborer's task is over, Now the battle day is past;
Now upon the farther shore Land the voyager at last.
There the tears of earth are dried;
There its hidden things are clear;
There the work of life is tried
By a greater judge than here.
"Earth to earth and dust to dust."
Calmly now the words we say;
Left behind, we wait in trust
For the resurrection day.
Father, in Thy gracious keeping
Leave we now Thy Servant Sleeping.
++++++++++++++++++++++]
"God shall wipe away all tears from their eyes; and there shall be no more death, neither **sorrow,** nor crying, neither shall there be any more pain...." Revelations 21:4

Rettie Huffmaster, October 3, 1973.

Carthage, Mo.--Mrs. Rettie Huffmaster, 87, Carthage Soute 4, died at 3:57 p.m. Wednesday at her home after a long illness. Mrs. Huffmaster was born September 2, 1886, in the State of Texas and lived most of her life In Elm Springs, Arkansas. She married Hal Harlan Huffmaster, July 8, 1906 at Elm Springs. He died February 3, 1963. She was a member of Missionary Baptist Church, Cave Springs, Arkansas

Survivors include three sons, J. W. Huffmaster, Carthage route 4, Martin Huffmaster, Springdale, Arkansas and J. B. Huffmaster, Moreauville, Lousiana; four daughters, Mrs. Mable Burton, Springdale, Mrs. Lelia Byrd, Fayetteville, Arkansas, Mrs. Ruby Burton, Pittsburg, Kansas and Mrs. Virginia Farrell, Willow Springs, Illinois; 3o grandchildren and several great-grandchildren. Services will be announced by Sisco Funeral Home, Springdale.

Lelia Byrd, 92, of Fayetteville died Sunday, Nov. 7, 2004, at Fayetteville Health and Rehabilitation Center. She was born Jan. 2, 1912, in Elm Springs to Hal and Rette George Huffmaster. She retired in 1995 from Matilda's on the Square after 40 years as a sales associate. She was active for many years in the Fayetteville Chapter of the Eastern Star and held numerous local and state offices. She was the church organist at Calvary Baptist Church for more than 30 years.

She was preceded in death by her husband, Sterling Byrd; her parents; and five siblings.

She is survived by a daughter, Elizabeth Byrd Glasco and her husband, Michael, of Dallas; a sister, Virginia

Farrell of Willow Springs, Ill.; and numerous nieces and nephews.

Visitation will be from 5 to 7 p.m. today at Moore's Chapel. Services will be at 2 p.m. Friday at Moore's Chapel with Dr. Gene Fulcher officiating. Burial will be in Goshen Cemetery. Memorials may be made to Alzheimer's Disease Research, 15825 Shady Grove Road, Suite 140, Rockville, Md., 20855; or Calvary Baptist Church Music Ministry, 1410 Porter Road, Fayetteville, 72703.

Betty Louise Mallard, 75, of Springdale, died Friday, Aug. 17, 2007, in Fayetteville. She was born Jan. 3, 1932, in Elm Springs, the daughter of Lewis and Mabel Huffmaster Burton. She was a retired supervisor of the trucking department for Tyson Foods and a Baptist. She is survived by one son, Charles Knox of Cypress, Texas, one brother, Jim Burton of Springdale, and two grandchildren. Funeral services will be Aug. 20 at 10 a. m. at Memorial Funeral Home in Springdale with the Rev. Tommy Poplin officiating. Burial will follow in Elm Springs Cemetery under the direction of Memorial Funeral Home. Visitation will be held today from 3 to 5 p. m. at the funeral home. Pallbearers will be Charles Knox, Rick Burton, Jerry Burton, Dwayne Burton, George Bagwell and Eric Bagwell

Tim A Cline, 31, of Rogers died February 6, 2001, at St. Mary's Hospital in Rogers. He was born February 12, 1969, in Little Rock to Cleburne Alvin and Darlene Huffmaster Cline. He was a musician, an artist and a waiter. He was a 1987 graduate of Rogers High School and was a member of Faith Assembly in Bentonville.

Survivors include two sons, Eric and Colton Cline,

both of Rogers; his parents of Rogers; one sister, Tammy Warren of Berryville; maternal grandmother, Ola Mae Williams of Springdale.

Services will be at 11 a.m. Friday at Burns Funeral Home in Rogers with Harley Hutcheson officiating. Burial will be in <u>Friendship Cemetery</u> in Springdale.

Visitation will be from 5 to 7 p.m. today at the funeral home. Memorials may be made to the Eric and Colton Cline Trust Fund, c/o Burns Funeral Home.

Pallbearers will be Gene Alberts, Jim Cline, I.R. Cline, Robert Cline, Danny Sams and Robert Sams. Honorary pallbearers will be Bill Warren, Martin Huffmaster, Eugene Cline and Mike Cline. *{mn}* <u>Rosa Cline</u>

Floyd J. Huffmaster

Floyd J. Huffmaster, 67, of Fayetteville, Ark., died Monday, May 31, 2004, at his home. He was born Sept. 20, 1936, in the Elm Springs/Cave Springs, Ark., area to William Huffmaster and Georgianne Downum Huffmaster. As a young child, he moved with his family to Bentonville, Ark., where he had a newspaper route and worked at Watkins Greenhouse. After graduating from high school, he worked at Kilby Sheet Metal, then for Neil Sheet Metal. He worked for Carlos Mayo Sheet Metal for almost 40 years. He was also a cattle farmer for 30 years.

He married Carolyn Edwards on June 6, 1958, in Senatobia, Miss. He was an active member of the Church of Christ in Johnson, Ark. He was an avid hunter and fisherman.

He was preceded in death by a son, Todd Huffmaster, in 1981.

Survivors include his wife, Carolyn Huffmaster;

a son and daughter-in-law, Terry Lee Huffmaster and Linda Rae Huffmaster of Fayetteville; three brothers, Lonnie Huffmaster of Independence, Mo., Darrell Huffmaster of Springdale, Ark., and *Billy Huffmaster of Pearl, Miss.; a sister, Francis Wright of Owensboro, Ky.; and three grandchildren, Heath Aaron Huffmaster, Laci Rae Huffmaster, and Lauren Mayhew and her husband Dustin Mayhew, all of Fayetteville.

Visitation will begin at noon Wednesday, June 2, at the Sisco Funeral Chapel in Springdale, Ark., with the family receiving friends from 5 p.m. to 7 p.m.

Funeral services will be at 2 p.m. Thursday, June 3, at the Church of Christ in Johnson, Ark., with Brother Gary Smith. Burial will be at the Stuckey Cemetery in Johnson.

Pallbearers will be Heath Huffmaster, Dustin Mayhew, David Cherry, Chuck Bluse, Tommy Smith and Virgil Harmon. Memorials may be made to Circle of Life Hospice, 601 E. Emma Ave., Springdale, AR 72764. *Billy is pastor of Baptist Church in Pearl, Mississippi.

(This is brother Bill's Grandson)

Daryl Huffmaster, 28, (formerly of Independence, Mo.) died January 12, 2007.

Daryl was born June 7, 1978 in Kansas City, Mo., the son of Leon and Jeannie (Hagler) Huffmaster. On June 24, 2000, he married Angela J. Copeland in Independence, Mo.

He was an automotive technician for Ricks Auto Clinic.

Survivors include his wife Angela; two daughters, Samantha Jo and Rachael Jean; son, Kyle Dennis, all of the home; mother, Jeannie Huffmaster, Oak Grove, Mo.; father, Leon Huffmaster, Bethany, Mo.; two brothers, Bryce Huffmaster, Oak Grove, Mo., and Lonnie Huffmaster, Independence, Mo.; grandfather, Lonnie Huffmaster, Independence, Mo.

Funeral services were Jan. 20, at the Roberson Funeral Home, Bethany, Mo., with Rev. Olin Slaughter officiating. Burial in Mt. Zion Cemetery, Bethany, Mo.

Memorials: Daryl Huffmaster Memorial Fund in care of the Roberson Funeral Home, P.O. Box 46, Bethany, Mo. 64424.

Mary M. Havens   Hal's Sister

Mrs. Mary M. Havens, 65, wife of Charles N. Havens of 0334 Massachusetts, died Monday at 12:25 p.m. in Newton Memorial hospital. She had been a patient there since Dec. 13th. Funeral services will be held at 2 p.m. Wednesday in the First Christian church with Rev. Glenn Shoemaker officiating. Burial will be in Tisdale cemetery with Swisher-Taylor funeral home in charge.

Mrs. Havens was born March 11, 1892 at Elm Springs, Ark., the daughter of Mr. and Mrs. John Huffmaster. She was married to Charles Havens April 20, 1921 at Elm Springs. She had been a resident of the Wilmot and Floral communities from 1921 until moving to Winfield in 1944. She was a member of the Christian Church and of the Army Mothers.

Survivors include her husband; two sons, Sherman L. of Arvin, Calif., and John W. of Winfield; two brothers, Hal and Joe Huffmaster of Springdale, Ark.; three sisters, Mrs. N. P. Norman of Eureka Springs, Ark., and Mrs.

Tom Harris of Springdale, Ark., and Mrs. A. C. Fogle of Denver.

Charlie N. Havens

Charlie N. Havens, of 0334 Massachusetts, died at 1:07 a.m. Tuesday at Newton Memorial hospital, where he had been admitted Monday.

He was born Jan. 5, 1895 in Washington County, Ark., the son of Mr. and Mrs. James W. Havens. He was brought to the Eaton community when 1 year old. The family later moved to the Wilmot community and since 1944 he had lived in Winfield.

He was married to Mary Huffmaster on April 20, 1921, at Fayetteville, Ark. She died Jan. 6, 1958. Survivors include 2 sons, Sherman of Arvin, Calif., and John of Winfield; a brother, Bert Havens, Wilmot, and 7 grandchildren.

He retired 3 years ago after service as a grain inspector for the U.S. Department of Agriculture. He was known to many as an old-time fiddler, especially at the time of the Kansas Centennial. Funeral arrangements will be announced by Swisher-Taylor funeral home.

C.L. George, Area Pountry pioneer dies. Charles Lee George 80, 702 Maple St. Springdale botn Frvrmnrt 19, 1888 in Elm Springs died May 26, 1969. He is survived by his wife, Mrs. Willie Lowe George, one son, Gene and one daughter, Mrs. Joe Redwine., 2 brothers, Maretin and Bill and one sister, Mrs. Hal Huffmaster of Elm Springs.

Doing a genealogy is like doing a jigsaw puzzle. Everyone's personality has unique ins and outs. I've read much where people just didn't always fit together. Here ends the saga of the Hoffmeister/Huffmaster family as I have found to date.

This is very evident when comparing the compassionate, caring Gottfried Hoffmaster to his brother Franz. Through out the research of Franz it is evident his personality causes him to have a problem. Eventually these problems put him on the run to save himself.

My opinion is that more of our ancestry are attuned to Gottfried's personality. Yetnone of them were found to be perfect; a black sheep can always be found----if the research is long and far enough into the past.

My opinion of the documents I have read, and there were many, if indeed we are not descendants of royalty, we certainly have many distinguished and reliable citizens of both Germany and the America's.

There are many grandchildren, nieces and nephews who are not mentioned. I have provided space at this end for you to record your family. Perhaps one day, someone will continue this document of the Hoffmeister/ Huffmaster genealogy starting with the 7th generation.

Dedication

This Novella is dedicated to all the ancestral fathers and to the present day heirs of the Hoffmeister/Huffmaster family. It has been a long journey of many generations to today.